T0064096

Love and Loss

Love and Loss

Michele Schlebach

LOVE AND LOSS

iUniverse books may be ordered through booksellers or by contacting:

iUniverse
1663 Liberty Drive
Bloomington, IN 47403
www.iuniverse.com
1-800-Authors (1-800-288-4677)

ISBN: 978-1-4917-4895-4 (sc)
ISBN: 978-1-4917-4896-1 (e)

Printed in the United States of America.

iUniverse rev. date: 10/03/2014

Dedication

This book is for some of the men and relationships I have had.
Some of the men are; Tim, Matt, Marcus, Wayne, Larry
and Frankie. Most have been over the last 5 years. If it wasn't
for these men, I couldn't have put my emotions in words.

━━━━━━━━━━━━━

Acknowledgments

Thanks to my sister, Amanda Miranda for helping me to be able to publish this book. She believed in me enough to help when I needed it. And thank you to a handful of people that also believed in me and encouraged me to keep with my dream of writing and sharing with others. Reading opens up different worlds and is an escape for many, myself included.

———∽∾∾⟨⟩∾∾∽———

From the depths of my heart and soul

I want to say thank you

You have been a breath of fresh air

Most people are fake

But you are real

You have been my sunshine everyday

Your smile is priceless

Whether we are lovers or friends

You have a place in my heart

If love was to blossom between us

You would search no more

You are my friend

And I will love you

For now and for always

———∽∾∾⟨⟩∾∾∽———

———❦❦❦———

I long to hold you
To kiss away the tears you shed
I want to use my fingers to trace
The outline of your face
To show you that I care

———❦❦❦———

—— ∾⊶⊙⊰⊙⊱⊙⊶∾ ——

To my prince charming
You are of pure heart and soul
When I hear your voice it moves me
You make even the coldest days warm
You make my inner soul sing of happiness
You bring promise into what was dismay

—— ∾⊶⊙⊰⊙⊱⊙⊶∾ ——

—————ᘉᘉᖆᘂᘉ⳥ᘂᘉᘉ—————

You are kind and tender

When you hold me

I feel safe and content

The whole world disappears

You are one of a kind

You are amazing

—————ᘉᘉᖆᘂᘉ⳥ᘂᘉᘉ—————

4

—∽∽∽◦◦◦❦◦◦◦∽∽∽—

You are my one and only

We have plenty of time to flourish

Whether it takes a week or months

You will see

I am true to you always

There is no other

And I am like no other you have seen

—∽∽∽◦◦◦❦◦◦◦∽∽∽—

———∽∾∿⁓⁓∿∾∽———

You are my prince in a world of frogs
I have waited for you for many days and nights
You ease my soul
And you fill me with happiness
I want to give you the joy you bring to me

———∽∾∿⁓⁓∿∾∽———

—∽∾⤳❦⤳∽∾—

You are amazing to me
The caring and tenderness I have seen

—∽∾⤳❦⤳∽∾—

—◦◦◦◦◦◦◦—

You deserve the happiness that you seek
I long to give it to you
To show you it does exist

—◦◦◦◦◦◦◦—

Your smile is beautiful

Like the sunshine that lights up the day

It brings me such joy

It is hard to explain

Your smile can make the worst of days bearable

Knowing your smile is waiting on me

———∿⌒◦◦⌒◦⌒◦◦⌒∿———

The hours are ticking by

The anticipation is killer

But all is worth its weight in gold

When we met I plan to keep what I hold

———∿⌒◦◦⌒◦⌒◦◦⌒∿———

—wooerooerooww—

My feelings are true

You will see

For my love will be true to thee

For all the pain we have been through

The time has come for love renewed

—wooerooerooww—

—∿∘⟲⟳∘⟳⟲∘∿—

Your touch makes me tremble
Your voice vibrates in my head
You have awaken feelings inside me
I hope one day you will return them
A new beginning is in store for you and I

—∿∘⟲⟳∘⟳⟲∘∿—

—∿∘∘⊙⊙⊙⊙∘∘∿—

I know you have been scorned
The stupidity of those women has soured you
But there is someone out there
A light that I can give you
Filled with hope and passion

—∿∘∘⊙⊙⊙⊙∘∘∿—

Sometimes in life

We are given what we need

Not always what we want

I am not what you are to us

Nor are you to me

But we were brought together for a reason

Feelings take time to develop

Fast ones fade

Slow ones grow

Know this

I am in for the long haul

Because I see the possibilities

———∼ᴍᴏᴏᴇᴛᴏᴏᴛᴇᴏᴏᴍ———

You have given me hope

To live again

To laugh again

To love again

That I may have a chance for happiness again

———∼ᴍᴏᴏᴇᴛᴏᴏᴛᴇᴏᴏᴍ———

———ⰉⰊⱁⰍⰃⰊⰃⰍⰃⰉⰊⱁ———

You are my love
You are my life
Your words comfort me
Your laughter brings me joy
My world is a better place with you in it

———ⰉⰊⱁⰍⰃⰊⰃⰍⰃⰉⰊⱁ———

—✦—✦✦✦—✦—

Because of you
I can see the sun through the haze
Because of you I can face the world
Knowing that you are by my side
Because of you
I feel love and hope to carry on

—✦—✦✦✦—✦—

—————ᘉᔊᘉᘍᘉᘍᔊᘉ—————

You are the air I breathe

Your every breath I take

Your love surrounds me with warmth

I am content and safe

—————ᘉᔊᘉᘍᘉᘍᔊᘉ—————

———〰︎∽◦◦❍◗✕◗❍◦◦∽〰︎———

To some you are

A devoted son

A loving father

A dependable brother

To others a great friend

To me you fill me with passion

Love

And a happy ending

———〰︎∽◦◦❍◗✕◗❍◦◦∽〰︎———

———ᴡᴏᴏᴇᴛᴏᴏᴋᴇᴏᴏᴡ———

The needs you fill for me are these

My friend

My confidant

My lover

My soul mate

Making my life worth living

———ᴡᴏᴏᴇᴛᴏᴏᴋᴇᴏᴏᴡ———

—————ᴡᴏ◦ᴄᴇᴛᴏᴄᴋᴇᴏ◦ᴡ—————

You have my heart

You have my soul

You are the sun that shines every day

You make my life complete

We are one together

—————ᴡᴏ◦ᴄᴇᴛᴏᴄᴋᴇᴏ◦ᴡ—————

———∽ຫ∽◦ຄຄ✕◇◇✕ຄຄ◦∽ຫ∽———

I want to lay down beside you every night

To hold you close and kiss you

Take away your worries and fears

To let you know my love is true

That I am here for you always

Loving you is easy for me

———∽ຫ∽◦ຄຄ✕◇◇✕ຄຄ◦∽ຫ∽———

———∿∿∘◦૯Ⓨ◐Ⓨ૯◦∘∿∿———

I dream of us

Our eyes meeting

Our lips touching

Our bodies feeling the warmth of each other

Our souls mating

Searching no more

I dream of us as one

———∿∿∘◦૯Ⓨ◐Ⓨ૯◦∘∿∿———

—❦———

You are the light at the end of the tunnel

When my day is in chaos

You soothe me with your words

And I return to sanity

Able to carry on

—❦———

What you are to me
You are the sun
You are the moon
You are the sky
You are the earth
The air I breathe is sweeter
What are you to me
My everything

———~ᴡᴏɢᴇᴛᴏᴏᴋᴇᴏᴏᴡ———

I thought about our meeting many times
But nothing compares to being in your arms
The love I felt and the safety you provided
Made me love and want you more
Our journey has just begun

———~ᴡᴏɢᴇᴛᴏᴏᴋᴇᴏᴏᴡ———

———www•o•o•oto•oto•oo•ww———

Loving you is easy
Your kisses are gentle
Your eyes look at me tenderly
Your heart is full of love for me
When I think of you I smile
You make every day worth living again

———www•o•o•oto•oto•oo•ww———

———〜〜〜———

You give me love
Peace and tranquility
When you say good morning
When you hold me
When you stroke my hair as I lay my head on you
When you say" I love you"
The times when you call me "baby girl"
Even when you say "Hey baby"
The way you kiss me when we are together
And when we make love
These are all the things you give me

———〜〜〜———

———～ⅿⅼⓐⓔⓣⓞⓞⓣⓔⓞⓞⅿ———

How do I know I'm in love with you
My heart skips a beat when you call
When I touch you I come alive
Talking to you makes me feel like a school girl
Kissing you excites me
Holding your hands gives me goose bumps
I dream of you all day long
I ache to be with you
I can't get enough of you
This is how I know I'm in love with you

———～ⅿⅼⓐⓔⓣⓞⓞⓣⓔⓞⓞⅿ———

—⁓⁓⁓⁓⁓⁓—

Breathe in
What do you smell
Love
Listen
What do you hear
Our hearts beating together
What do you feel
Time standing still
Look
What do you see
Beauty at our union

—⁓⁓⁓⁓⁓⁓—

—wooensokeoom—

You are my first thought when I open my eyes
You are my last thought when I close my eyes
During the day I think of your smile
Of your laugh
Thoughts of our time together
Thoughts of what our future
And all that will be in between
You begin my day
And end my nights

—wooensokeoom—

———~ᴡ∘₰₰₰∘~———

You make my day
So much better
You make the sunshine
Even on a gloomy day

———~ᴡ∘₰₰₰∘~———

———∿∿°◦℮ↄↃ⊙ↄↃ℮◦°∿∿———

What is friendship

Caring

Sharing

Listening

Being there for each other

Calling to say "Hello"

Being a shoulder to cry on

Not judging

Talking in the middle of the night

When you are hurting

Giving yourself unconditionally

Being the last one standing

As I will surely be for you

———∿∿°◦℮ↄↃ⊙ↄↃ℮◦°∿∿———

———～mo⌒℮⌒↦℮⌒o⌒ww———

Complicated

That is what we are

Your worries

Your failures

Your worries of commitment

Let yourself be free

Love is here

Waiting to develop

Take it

Run with it

Doubt no more

Your answer is here with me

———～mo⌒℮⌒↦℮⌒o⌒ww———

In you

I see my heart

The light that shines

In eyes that mean everything to me

There is nothing you can do

That makes me think any other way

Because to me you mean everything

—⁓⁓⋯⁓⁓—

I feel it

The connection is there

The true friendship we share

Whether we talk every day or not

We share

We laugh

We have even cried to each other

We enjoy our time together

The way it should be

You are on my mind

And are in my heart always

You will forever be with me

—⁓⁓⋯⁓⁓—

———〜〜◦◦❦❧◦◦〜〜———

Know this
There will never be too many miles
Nor never too late to call
I will always come to you

———〜〜◦◦❦❧◦◦〜〜———

———∽∾♥∾∽———

Any day spent with you is a gift
The minutes with you are precious
Listening to you breathe
Hearing your heart beat
Lying next to you
Sharing coffee with you in the early morning
Memories that can't be replaced
Instilled in me
I'm here for you now
I will be here for you now and til the end

———∽∾♥∾∽———

———～◦◦◦◦◦◦～———

Dazed and confused
Is the way life is today
Not knowing our feelings
Emotions
Actions
Not knowing our next move
People asking too much of us
Relax
Breathe
Choices are made daily
But some change comes in time
Know that in the end
I will be here to catch you if you fall

———～◦◦◦◦◦◦～———

—wooↄↄↄↄↄↄↄↄoↄↄↄ—

Kendered spirits
That is what we are
Sharing the same beliefs
Attitudes
Feelings about life
That others do not understand
To reconnect after many years
Has made my life surreal
You have awaken me
To the things I had thought were lost

—wooↄↄↄↄↄↄↄↄoↄↄↄ—

———ᴡᴏᴏᴄᴛᴏᴏᴛᴏᴏᴡ———

You are the sunshine and light of each day

The colorful rainbow in the sky

You are my want and my need in one

My passion and joy

Your scars run deep

I want to help heal them

Do not dwell or return to the past

Think of the future

What could be

It is within your reach

Grasp it

Hold on to it

For it is yours

As am I

———ᴡᴏᴏᴄᴛᴏᴏᴛᴏᴏᴡ———

———～ハ○の○*○○*○○ハ～———

Lovers intertwined

Emotions

Hearts

Souls

Bodies

Becoming one

Bonding

Sharing

Seeing nothing

Just each other

———～ハ○の○*○○*○○ハ～———

—wooooooooo—

I want to run my fingers through your hair
Trace your lips with my fingertips
Feel your hot skin against mine
Heart your heartbeat
As I lay my head on your chest
Listening to your breathing in the darkness
As we fall asleep in each other's arms

—wooooooooo—

———∽∾⧜∾∽———

What you do to me
Your smile is hypnotizing
Your eyes are piercing
Your kisses make me melt
When you touch me my skin tingles
When we are lying together I feel at peace and content
This is an awesome feeling what you do to me

———∽∾⧜∾∽———

—————~mⵜⵗⵗ~—————

Oceans of darkness and pain have consumed you

But the waters are calming

There are blue skies and sun shine ahead

The light is just in your grasp

I hope I am part of your new beginning

—————~mⵜⵗⵗ~—————

———woooooooooow———

You are the sunshine that makes my day
You are the rainbow after the rain
Our conversations engulf me
This is real
This is friendship and so much more

———woooooooooow———

I like you for you

Your humor

Your wit

Your laugh

Your zest for life

This attracts me

———〰∘◦❦❧◦∘〰———

Lost spirits

Finding each other again

After many years and days passed

But the time is right for reconnection

Others do not understand

Nor could they

———〰∘◦❦❧◦∘〰———

It is a hot and humid night
The moon is full
Where are you I call
Nothing
I wonder around aimlessly
Finding a willow tree
I can smell you
Your sent is strong
You are toying with me
Making me want you more
I pull the canopy drapes apart
I can barely see you
Lying on the ground
As I near you
You pull me to you
We lie on the ground
Under the tree
Staring in to each other's eyes
We are scadly dressed
Touching each other lightly
Then the primal animal instinct takes over
We are lost in each other
Our minds
Souls and bodies
Becoming one until sated
We lie until dawn
Under the willow tree

—⁓⁓⁓⁓⁓—

I am at a loss
Understanding decreases everyday
Why have you shut me out
Communication was good
Connecting almost as one
I was in a dark place
But you brought light and sunshine
The sun has since regressed

—⁓⁓⁓⁓⁓—

———∽∾∿⌒⌒∿∾∽———

Every day I lose a piece of me

My soul

My faith

Life laughs

Dangling what could be in my face

When sunlight was surfacing

Darkness found its way passed

Stealing any happiness I had seen

Leaving me empty

Cold

Unsure of what lies ahead

Not seeing beyond the darkness

Turning my heart to stone

Leaving what could be

Unreachable

———∽∾∿⌒⌒∿∾∽———

—wooeroeoroom—

You come back time and again
Always the same thing
Wanting physical release
No mental attachments
Leaving me empty
While you are fulfilled
Not caring about the toll it takes on me
The state I am left in
The ball of emotions rolling around
This is why I keep my distance
This is why we will never be

—wooeroeoroom—

—∿⌒☙❦☙⌒∿—

I believed in you

Thought you were going to be different

You started out with promises that gave me hope

Our time was short lived

You said maybe at a later date

But there won't be any

Your chance is gone

Like the hopes of us

—∿⌒☙❦☙⌒∿—

———∿∾⊙⨯⊙⨯⊙∾∿———

Numb

You ask me why I am numb

I should feel alive

But I don't

I feel alive around you

Your energy and insight feeds me

Others do not compare

Go

Seek

Find

Your confusion is far from over

As my numbness grows with it

———∿∾⊙⨯⊙⨯⊙∾∿———

———ᴡᴏᴏᴄᴛᴏᴏᴛᴏᴏᴡ———

I will wait

If only for a bit

I will bide my time

Stand in the shadows

But yet

Surprise you when you aren't expecting it

Keep me close in thought

Because one day I could be gone like a thief in the night

———ᴡᴏᴏᴄᴛᴏᴏᴛᴏᴏᴡ———

—————ᴟᴑᴑᴇᴛᴑ⊙ᴛᴇᴑᴑᴟᴟ—————

Tears have filled my eyes
They roll down like a river
The pain is real
The story of my life
They say your awesome
But that doesn't matter
Awesome is just a word
Words are empty
Actions are real
Seeing is believing
Isn't that what they say
So what is left loneness

—————ᴟᴑᴑᴇᴛᴑ⊙ᴛᴇᴑᴑᴟᴟ—————

—⁓ⲟⲟⲉⲧⲟⲟⲧⲟⲟⲱⲱ—

You made a mistake letting me go
Not waiting for what was in the future
Your Impatience won
But I will always be on your mind
My raven hair and face will haunt you
I will stir a storm in your dreams and in your thoughts
Making it difficult for you to forget me
I have cursed you
Your darkest hour has yet to fall

—⁓ⲟⲟⲉⲧⲟⲟⲧⲟⲟⲱⲱ—

—∿∿∘⌒⌒⌒⌒⌒⌒∘∿∿—

I feel like I'm in a hurricane
Our relationship is on the outside
Emotions whipping back and forth
Then it goes calm
Like the center
Settled and quite
Then the winds come back again
Leaving destruction in its path

—∿∿∘⌒⌒⌒⌒⌒⌒∘∿∿—

—〰️➰➰➰〰️—

Confused
Confusion fills my mind
Sometimes you are hot
Sometimes you are cold
You talk to me
Then silence
I have given you my all
Confessed my love to you
At times I am at a loss
What have I done
Then you speak
And I am taken in again
Making me confused again
To wonder what is next

—〰️➰➰➰〰️—

＊＊＊

I fell hard
I fell fast
You are everything I wanted
At first all the signs were there
But after
I could tell that things have changed

＊＊＊

———∾∾∾∽∾∾∾———

I have seen the signs over the last few weeks

The difference in you

The talks have been short

The "I love you" not as much

The hesitation in your voice

Why

I ask myself

The answers you give are confusing

———∾∾∾∽∾∾∾———

———∿∾ᖇᘖᘖᘖᘖᘖᘖᖇᘖ∾∿———

I am numb
My heart bleeds
Your struggle with our commitments
I am sorry that what comes easy for me
Is so hard for you
The tears won't stop
To think what we have will be over soon

———∿∾ᖇᘖᘖᘖᘖᘖᘖᖇᘖ∾∿———

———∿∘๑ᏋᎿᎪᎿᏋ๑∘∿———

I keep hearing your voice whisper

The whispers of laughter

Laughter at me

What a fool I was

Believing you really cared and wanted me

It was just a game to you

But my feeling were real

Now those feelings are forever locked away

———∿∘๑ᏋᎿᎪᎿᏋ๑∘∿———

—wooerooteoow—

You cut me open with a knife
I keep bleeding love
The love that could have been yours
The bleeding is spilling on my chest
My heart is draining dry
Because that's how you left me
High and dry

—wooerooteoow—

———ᴡᴏᴏᴄᴇᴛᴏᴏᴛᴇᴏᴏᴡ———

You have been lied to and cheated on
I offered you a pure and loving heart
You rejected it
Without thought or feeling
Discarded like a piece of paper
To blow in the wind
Like trash on the street

———ᴡᴏᴏᴄᴇᴛᴏᴏᴛᴇᴏᴏᴡ———

———❦❦❦———

You were my fantasy
You were my world
For two days my bliss was unreal
I hung on your every word
My feelings were growing stronger
Then my world fell apart
I am dying a little each day

———❦❦❦———

—wooeoooeoow—

You said one time
You hoped my feelings were real
They were
They are
Yet I tried to show you
And you never returned them
I did not realize
Until I was alone
That all was just misunderstood
Your intentions were not the same as mine

—wooeoooeoow—

———∽∾∽◦∾◦∽∽∾∽———

There are times when I can't breathe

Thinking of how much I miss you

Wondering if I ever cross your mind

Wanting you so bad that my heart fills like it will explode

Knowing I am just kidding myself

———∽∾∽◦∾◦∽∽∾∽———

———∿∘᛭᛭᛭∘∿———

You hit me like a summer storm

The wind blew

The ground shook

And I was blinded by the lightening

All of the emotions hit me a t once

But then ended like a tornado

Nothing but disaster left of my heart

———∿∘᛭᛭᛭∘∿———

———∿∘⟨⟩∘⟨⟩∘∿———

I remember those nights in your arms

Laying there listening to you breathe

The contentment and joy I felt

I miss those nights desperately

The longing for you is unbearable

———∿∘⟨⟩∘⟨⟩∘∿———

My heart was broken today
You didn't have to say it
I saw it with my own eyes
My feelings were running deep
But you were running away
The truth would have been better
Than the waiting

———～ᴡ∘৹ᴇ৹⊛৹ᴇ৹∘ᴡ———

I wanted you to be my everything

The talks we had

The laughter we shared

All the signs were there

The possibilities were endless

Then "Bam" you were gone

———～ᴡ∘৹ᴇ৹⊛৹ᴇ৹∘ᴡ———

———∿∾⚬⚭⚮⚭⚬∾∿———

I offered you my heart and soul
But you rejected it
You did not see the stars in my eyes
The stars I longed to give you
The stars that would have made us one

———∿∾⚬⚭⚮⚭⚬∾∿———

—wooooooooow—

You are still special to me
No matter how many miles separate us
I am just a phone call away
I am here for you
I long to hold you
Even though it will never be

—wooooooooow—

When I first saw you my heart skipped a beat
Wondering what you would see in me
When you talked to me I was in awe
My heart grew fonder of you
And yours less of me
I can see I was just dreaming

———∿∽◦◟◝◜◞◝◜◞◦∽∿———

I wanted you

Not for what you have

But for who you showed me you were

You showed me your sweet side

That later turned mean

I am confused

I am hurt

Recovery is far from over

———∿∽◦◟◝◜◞◝◜◞◦∽∿———

—◦◦◦—

Today you broke my heart
It was not with words but with actions
I tried to show you what real caring is
Yet you threw it away
I tried to show you what real love could be
I would have never given myself to you
Had I known the outcome

—◦◦◦—

My heart is in turmoil
Not knowing your side
I expressed the yearning for you
With no return
Sometimes the silence is deafening
I am screaming inside

Even in death you haunt me
With your approaching anniversary this increases
The dreams more often
I wake weeping
With memories of us
Some good
Some bad
We were like fire and gasoline
That fine line between love and hate
Trying to stay apart
But always returning
Then it happened
You were gone
We never said good-bye
Will I ever have closure
Or will you forever be my ghost

———～ᨏᨏᨏᨏᨏᨏᨏᨏ———

My days have been empty
My nights have been hell
Not knowing why
What happened
It has been 4 days since we last talked
The torture is killing me
The silence is unnerving

———～ᨏᨏᨏᨏᨏᨏᨏᨏ———

—∿∿⌒⌒⌒⌒⌒⌒∿∿—

We reap what we sow

We are told

So beware

Karma is coming

Remember the cut open bleeding heart you left

Wounded

Alone

To heal on its own

Has taken residence in a dark place

A cold place

A place it has been many times before

So be warmed of the thoughts coming your way

Dark

Sad

Lonely

I will be in your thoughts

Your dreams

Your sleep

Haunting you

The demons will not rest

Reap it

Reap it

—∿∿⌒⌒⌒⌒⌒⌒∿∿—

—◦◦◦—

You come to me in the darkness,
When I am sleeping,
When I am alone,
In my dreams when I am weakest,
Showing me the good times,
That we loved each other deeply,
But when I wake I am weaping,
Because you are gone,
Two years now,
And I will never see you again,
You are gone,
Forever . . . .

—◦◦◦—

———❦———

About the Author

Michele Schlebach, I am 47 years old, divorced and I live in Jacksonville, Arkansas. I have one daughter, who is 27 years old, and 4 grandsons. I am currently a pet groomer. In my spare time I like to read and write. I also have a bachelor's degree in Social and Criminal Justice.

———❦———